THIS BOOK BELONGS TO:

CONTACT INFORMATION

NAME:	
ADDRESS:	
PHONE:	

START / END DATES

_____ / _____ / _____ TO _____ / _____ / _____

DEDICATION

This Photographer Journal is dedicated to all the photographers out there who love to capture special moments and document their findings in the process.

You are my inspiration for producing books and I'm honored to be a part of keeping all of your Photography notes and records organized.

This journal notebook will help you record your details about tracking your photo sessions.

Thoughtfully put together with these sections to record: Date & Time, Image #, Shooting Mode, Meter Mode, In-Camera Settings, Weather, Lighting Description, & Shot Notes.

HOW TO USE THIS BOOK

The purpose of this book is to keep all of your Photographer notes all in one place. It will help keep you organized.

This Photographer Journal will allow you to accurately document every detail about your photo sessions. It's a great way to chart your course through an amazing photo shoot.

Here are examples of the prompts for you to fill in and write about your experience in this book:

1. **Date & Time** - Write the date and time of the photoshoot.

2. **Image #** - Log the image number.

3. **Shooting Mode** - Record ISO, WB, Aperture, Shutter Speed, & Tripod Used.

4. **Meter Mode** - Write EV +/-, Lens, Focal Length, Flash, Flash Settings.

5. **In-Camera Settings** - Log setting specific to your camera.

6. **Weather** - Record what the weather is like.

7. **Lighting Description** - Describe your lighting.

8. **Shot Notes** - Blank lined for writing any other important notes such as landscape/ nature, headshots, family, wedding, studios, portrait photos, senior pictures, black and white, newborn baby session, fashion shoot, the goal for the shoot, etc.

PHOTOGRAPHY LOGBOOK

DATE		TIME		○ AM ○ PM
IMAGE #				

SHOOTING MODE		METER MODE		
ISO		EV +/-		
WB		LENS		VR ○ ON ○ OFF
APERTURE		FOCAL LENGTH		
SHUTTER SPEED		FLASH	○ YES ○ NO	
TRIPOD	○ YES ○ NO	FLASH SETTINGS		

IN CAMERA SETTINGS	WEATHER

LIGHTING DESCRIPTION

SHOT NOTES

PHOTOGRAPHY LOGBOOK

DATE		TIME		○ AM ○ PM
IMAGE #				

SHOOTING MODE		METER MODE			
ISO		EV +/-			
WB		LENS		VR	○ ON ○ OFF
APERTURE		FOCAL LENGTH			
SHUTTER SPEED		FLASH	○ YES ○ NO		
TRIPOD	○ YES ○ NO	FLASH SETTINGS			

IN CAMERA SETTINGS	WEATHER

LIGHTING DESCRIPTION

SHOT NOTES

PHOTOGRAPHY LOGBOOK

DATE		TIME		○ AM ○ PM
IMAGE #				

SHOOTING MODE		METER MODE		
ISO		EV +/-		
WB		LENS		VR ○ ON ○ OFF
APERTURE		FOCAL LENGTH		
SHUTTER SPEED		FLASH	○ YES ○ NO	
TRIPOD	○ YES ○ NO	FLASH SETTINGS		

IN CAMERA SETTINGS	WEATHER

LIGHTING DESCRIPTION

SHOT NOTES

PHOTOGRAPHY LOGBOOK

DATE		TIME		○ AM ○ PM
IMAGE #				

SHOOTING MODE		METER MODE		
ISO		EV +/-		
WB		LENS		VR ○ ON ○ OFF
APERTURE		FOCAL LENGTH		
SHUTTER SPEED		FLASH	○ YES ○ NO	
TRIPOD	○ YES ○ NO	FLASH SETTINGS		

IN CAMERA SETTINGS	WEATHER

LIGHTING DESCRIPTION

SHOT NOTES

PHOTOGRAPHY LOGBOOK

DATE		TIME		○ AM ○ PM
IMAGE #				

SHOOTING MODE		METER MODE			
ISO		EV +/-			
WB		LENS		VR	○ ON ○ OFF
APERTURE		FOCAL LENGTH			
SHUTTER SPEED		FLASH	○ YES ○ NO		
TRIPOD	○ YES ○ NO	FLASH SETTINGS			

IN CAMERA SETTINGS	WEATHER

LIGHTING DESCRIPTION

SHOT NOTES

PHOTOGRAPHY LOGBOOK

DATE		TIME		○ AM ○ PM
IMAGE #				

SHOOTING MODE		METER MODE		
ISO		EV +/-		
WB		LENS		VR ○ ON ○ OFF
APERTURE		FOCAL LENGTH		
SHUTTER SPEED		FLASH	○ YES ○ NO	
TRIPOD	○ YES ○ NO	FLASH SETTINGS		

IN CAMERA SETTINGS	WEATHER

LIGHTING DESCRIPTION

SHOT NOTES

PHOTOGRAPHY LOGBOOK

DATE		TIME		○ AM ○ PM
IMAGE #				

SHOOTING MODE		METER MODE		
ISO		EV +/-		
WB		LENS		VR ○ ON ○ OFF
APERTURE		FOCAL LENGTH		
SHUTTER SPEED		FLASH	○ YES ○ NO	
TRIPOD	○ YES ○ NO	FLASH SETTINGS		

IN CAMERA SETTINGS	WEATHER

LIGHTING DESCRIPTION

SHOT NOTES

PHOTOGRAPHY LOGBOOK

DATE		TIME		○ AM ○ PM
IMAGE #				

SHOOTING MODE		METER MODE		
ISO		EV +/-		
WB		LENS		VR ○ ON ○ OFF
APERTURE		FOCAL LENGTH		
SHUTTER SPEED		FLASH	○ YES ○ NO	
TRIPOD	○ YES ○ NO	FLASH SETTINGS		

IN CAMERA SETTINGS

WEATHER

LIGHTING DESCRIPTION

SHOT NOTES

PHOTOGRAPHY LOGBOOK

DATE		TIME		○ AM ○ PM
IMAGE #				

SHOOTING MODE		METER MODE			
ISO		EV +/-			
WB		LENS		VR	○ ON ○ OFF
APERTURE		FOCAL LENGTH			
SHUTTER SPEED		FLASH	○ YES ○ NO		
TRIPOD	○ YES ○ NO	FLASH SETTINGS			

IN CAMERA SETTINGS	WEATHER

LIGHTING DESCRIPTION

SHOT NOTES

PHOTOGRAPHY LOGBOOK

DATE		TIME		○ AM ○ PM
IMAGE #				

SHOOTING MODE		METER MODE		
ISO		EV +/-		
WB		LENS	VR	○ ON ○OFF
APERTURE		FOCAL LENGTH		
SHUTTER SPEED		FLASH	○ YES ○ NO	
TRIPOD	○ YES ○ NO	FLASH SETTINGS		

IN CAMERA SETTINGS	WEATHER

LIGHTING DESCRIPTION

SHOT NOTES

PHOTOGRAPHY LOGBOOK

DATE		TIME		○ AM ○ PM
IMAGE #				

SHOOTING MODE		METER MODE	
ISO		EV +/-	
WB		LENS	VR ○ ON ○ OFF
APERTURE		FOCAL LENGTH	
SHUTTER SPEED		FLASH	○ YES ○ NO
TRIPOD	○ YES ○ NO	FLASH SETTINGS	

IN CAMERA SETTINGS	WEATHER

LIGHTING DESCRIPTION

SHOT NOTES

PHOTOGRAPHY LOGBOOK

DATE		TIME		○ AM ○ PM
IMAGE #				

SHOOTING MODE		METER MODE		
ISO		EV +/-		
WB		LENS		VR ○ ON ○ OFF
APERTURE		FOCAL LENGTH		
SHUTTER SPEED		FLASH	○ YES ○ NO	
TRIPOD	○ YES ○ NO	FLASH SETTINGS		

IN CAMERA SETTINGS	WEATHER

LIGHTING DESCRIPTION

SHOT NOTES

PHOTOGRAPHY LOGBOOK

DATE		TIME		○ AM ○ PM
IMAGE #				

SHOOTING MODE		METER MODE			
ISO		EV +/-			
WB		LENS		VR	○ ON ○ OFF
APERTURE		FOCAL LENGTH			
SHUTTER SPEED		FLASH	○ YES ○ NO		
TRIPOD	○ YES ○ NO	FLASH SETTINGS			

IN CAMERA SETTINGS	WEATHER

LIGHTING DESCRIPTION

SHOT NOTES

PHOTOGRAPHY LOGBOOK

DATE		TIME		○ AM ○ PM
IMAGE #				

SHOOTING MODE		METER MODE		
ISO		EV +/-		
WB		LENS		VR ○ ON ○ OFF
APERTURE		FOCAL LENGTH		
SHUTTER SPEED		FLASH	○ YES ○ NO	
TRIPOD	○ YES ○ NO	FLASH SETTINGS		

IN CAMERA SETTINGS

WEATHER

LIGHTING DESCRIPTION

SHOT NOTES

PHOTOGRAPHY LOGBOOK

DATE		TIME		○ AM ○ PM
IMAGE #				

SHOOTING MODE		METER MODE		
ISO		EV +/-		
WB		LENS		VR ○ ON ○ OFF
APERTURE		FOCAL LENGTH		
SHUTTER SPEED		FLASH	○ YES ○ NO	
TRIPOD	○ YES ○ NO	FLASH SETTINGS		

IN CAMERA SETTINGS	WEATHER

LIGHTING DESCRIPTION

SHOT NOTES

PHOTOGRAPHY LOGBOOK

DATE		TIME		○ AM ○ PM
IMAGE #				

SHOOTING MODE		METER MODE		
ISO		EV +/-		
WB		LENS	VR	○ ON ○ OFF
APERTURE		FOCAL LENGTH		
SHUTTER SPEED		FLASH	○ YES ○ NO	
TRIPOD	○ YES ○ NO	FLASH SETTINGS		

IN CAMERA SETTINGS	WEATHER

LIGHTING DESCRIPTION

SHOT NOTES

PHOTOGRAPHY LOGBOOK

DATE		TIME		○ AM ○ PM
IMAGE #				

SHOOTING MODE		METER MODE		
ISO		EV +/-		
WB		LENS		VR ○ ON ○ OFF
APERTURE		FOCAL LENGTH		
SHUTTER SPEED		FLASH	○ YES ○ NO	
TRIPOD	○ YES ○ NO	FLASH SETTINGS		

IN CAMERA SETTINGS	WEATHER

LIGHTING DESCRIPTION

SHOT NOTES

PHOTOGRAPHY LOGBOOK

DATE		TIME		○ AM ○ PM
IMAGE #				

SHOOTING MODE		METER MODE		
ISO		EV +/-		
WB		LENS		VR ○ ON ○ OFF
APERTURE		FOCAL LENGTH		
SHUTTER SPEED		FLASH	○ YES ○ NO	
TRIPOD	○ YES ○ NO	FLASH SETTINGS		

IN CAMERA SETTINGS	WEATHER

LIGHTING DESCRIPTION

SHOT NOTES

PHOTOGRAPHY LOGBOOK

DATE		TIME		○ AM ○ PM
IMAGE #				

SHOOTING MODE		METER MODE		
ISO		EV +/-		
WB		LENS		VR ○ ON ○ OFF
APERTURE		FOCAL LENGTH		
SHUTTER SPEED		FLASH	○ YES ○ NO	
TRIPOD	○ YES ○ NO	FLASH SETTINGS		

IN CAMERA SETTINGS	WEATHER

LIGHTING DESCRIPTION

SHOT NOTES

PHOTOGRAPHY LOGBOOK

DATE		TIME		○ AM ○ PM
IMAGE #				

SHOOTING MODE		METER MODE		
ISO		EV +/-		
WB		LENS		VR ○ ON ○ OFF
APERTURE		FOCAL LENGTH		
SHUTTER SPEED		FLASH	○ YES ○ NO	
TRIPOD	○ YES ○ NO	FLASH SETTINGS		

IN CAMERA SETTINGS	WEATHER

LIGHTING DESCRIPTION

SHOT NOTES

PHOTOGRAPHY LOGBOOK

DATE		TIME		○ AM ○ PM
IMAGE #				

SHOOTING MODE		METER MODE		
ISO		EV +/-		
WB		LENS	VR	○ ON ○ OFF
APERTURE		FOCAL LENGTH		
SHUTTER SPEED		FLASH	○ YES ○ NO	
TRIPOD	○ YES ○ NO	FLASH SETTINGS		

IN CAMERA SETTINGS	WEATHER

LIGHTING DESCRIPTION

SHOT NOTES

PHOTOGRAPHY LOGBOOK

DATE		TIME		○ AM ○ PM
IMAGE #				

SHOOTING MODE		METER MODE		
ISO		EV +/-		
WB		LENS		VR ○ ON ○ OFF
APERTURE		FOCAL LENGTH		
SHUTTER SPEED		FLASH	○ YES ○ NO	
TRIPOD	○ YES ○ NO	FLASH SETTINGS		

IN CAMERA SETTINGS	WEATHER

LIGHTING DESCRIPTION

SHOT NOTES

PHOTOGRAPHY LOGBOOK

DATE		TIME		○ AM ○ PM
IMAGE #				

SHOOTING MODE		METER MODE			
ISO		EV +/-			
WB		LENS		VR	○ ON ○ OFF
APERTURE		FOCAL LENGTH			
SHUTTER SPEED		FLASH	○ YES ○ NO		
TRIPOD	○ YES ○ NO	FLASH SETTINGS			

IN CAMERA SETTINGS

WEATHER

LIGHTING DESCRIPTION

SHOT NOTES

PHOTOGRAPHY LOGBOOK

DATE		TIME		○ AM ○ PM
IMAGE #				

SHOOTING MODE		METER MODE		
ISO		EV +/-		
WB		LENS		VR ○ ON ○ OFF
APERTURE		FOCAL LENGTH		
SHUTTER SPEED		FLASH	○ YES ○ NO	
TRIPOD	○ YES ○ NO	FLASH SETTINGS		

IN CAMERA SETTINGS	WEATHER

LIGHTING DESCRIPTION

SHOT NOTES

PHOTOGRAPHY LOGBOOK

DATE		TIME		○ AM ○ PM
IMAGE #				

SHOOTING MODE		METER MODE			
ISO		EV +/-			
WB		LENS		VR	○ ON ○ OFF
APERTURE		FOCAL LENGTH			
SHUTTER SPEED		FLASH	○ YES ○ NO		
TRIPOD	○ YES ○ NO	FLASH SETTINGS			

IN CAMERA SETTINGS

WEATHER

LIGHTING DESCRIPTION

SHOT NOTES

PHOTOGRAPHY LOGBOOK

DATE		TIME		○ AM ○ PM
IMAGE #				

SHOOTING MODE		METER MODE		
ISO		EV +/-		
WB		LENS		VR ○ ON ○ OFF
APERTURE		FOCAL LENGTH		
SHUTTER SPEED		FLASH	○ YES ○ NO	
TRIPOD	○ YES ○ NO	FLASH SETTINGS		

IN CAMERA SETTINGS	WEATHER

LIGHTING DESCRIPTION

SHOT NOTES

PHOTOGRAPHY LOGBOOK

DATE		TIME		○ AM ○ PM
IMAGE #				

SHOOTING MODE		METER MODE		
ISO		EV +/−		
WB		LENS		VR ○ ON ○ OFF
APERTURE		FOCAL LENGTH		
SHUTTER SPEED		FLASH	○ YES ○ NO	
TRIPOD	○ YES ○ NO	FLASH SETTINGS		

IN CAMERA SETTINGS	WEATHER

LIGHTING DESCRIPTION

SHOT NOTES

PHOTOGRAPHY LOGBOOK

DATE		TIME		○ AM ○ PM
IMAGE #				

SHOOTING MODE		METER MODE		
ISO		EV +/-		
WB		LENS	VR	○ ON ○ OFF
APERTURE		FOCAL LENGTH		
SHUTTER SPEED		FLASH	○ YES ○ NO	
TRIPOD	○ YES ○ NO	FLASH SETTINGS		

IN CAMERA SETTINGS	WEATHER

LIGHTING DESCRIPTION

SHOT NOTES

PHOTOGRAPHY LOGBOOK

DATE		TIME		○ AM ○ PM
IMAGE #				

SHOOTING MODE		METER MODE		
ISO		EV +/-		
WB		LENS		VR ○ ON ○ OFF
APERTURE		FOCAL LENGTH		
SHUTTER SPEED		FLASH	○ YES ○ NO	
TRIPOD	○ YES ○ NO	FLASH SETTINGS		

IN CAMERA SETTINGS	WEATHER

LIGHTING DESCRIPTION

SHOT NOTES

PHOTOGRAPHY LOGBOOK

DATE		TIME		○ AM ○ PM
IMAGE #				

SHOOTING MODE		METER MODE		
ISO		EV +/-		
WB		LENS		VR ○ ON ○ OFF
APERTURE		FOCAL LENGTH		
SHUTTER SPEED		FLASH	○ YES ○ NO	
TRIPOD	○ YES ○ NO	FLASH SETTINGS		

IN CAMERA SETTINGS	WEATHER

LIGHTING DESCRIPTION

SHOT NOTES

PHOTOGRAPHY LOGBOOK

DATE		TIME		○ AM ○ PM
IMAGE #				

SHOOTING MODE		METER MODE		
ISO		EV +/-		
WB		LENS		VR ○ ON ○ OFF
APERTURE		FOCAL LENGTH		
SHUTTER SPEED		FLASH	○ YES ○ NO	
TRIPOD	○ YES ○ NO	FLASH SETTINGS		

IN CAMERA SETTINGS	WEATHER

LIGHTING DESCRIPTION

SHOT NOTES

PHOTOGRAPHY LOGBOOK

DATE		TIME		○ AM ○ PM
IMAGE #				

SHOOTING MODE		METER MODE			
ISO		EV +/-			
WB		LENS		VR	○ ON ○ OFF
APERTURE		FOCAL LENGTH			
SHUTTER SPEED		FLASH	○ YES ○ NO		
TRIPOD	○ YES ○ NO	FLASH SETTINGS			

IN CAMERA SETTINGS	WEATHER

LIGHTING DESCRIPTION

SHOT NOTES

PHOTOGRAPHY LOGBOOK

DATE		TIME		○ AM ○ PM
IMAGE #				

SHOOTING MODE		METER MODE		
ISO		EV +/-		
WB		LENS		VR ○ ON ○ OFF
APERTURE		FOCAL LENGTH		
SHUTTER SPEED		FLASH	○ YES ○ NO	
TRIPOD	○ YES ○ NO	FLASH SETTINGS		

IN CAMERA SETTINGS	WEATHER

LIGHTING DESCRIPTION

SHOT NOTES

PHOTOGRAPHY LOGBOOK

DATE		TIME		○ AM ○ PM
IMAGE #				

SHOOTING MODE		METER MODE		
ISO		EV +/-		
WB		LENS		VR ○ ON ○ OFF
APERTURE		FOCAL LENGTH		
SHUTTER SPEED		FLASH	○ YES ○ NO	
TRIPOD	○ YES ○ NO	FLASH SETTINGS		

IN CAMERA SETTINGS	WEATHER

LIGHTING DESCRIPTION

SHOT NOTES

PHOTOGRAPHY LOGBOOK

DATE		TIME		○ AM ○ PM
IMAGE #				

SHOOTING MODE		METER MODE		
ISO		EV +/-		
WB		LENS		VR ○ ON ○ OFF
APERTURE		FOCAL LENGTH		
SHUTTER SPEED		FLASH	○ YES ○ NO	
TRIPOD	○ YES ○ NO	FLASH SETTINGS		

IN CAMERA SETTINGS	WEATHER

LIGHTING DESCRIPTION

SHOT NOTES

PHOTOGRAPHY LOGBOOK

DATE		TIME		○ AM ○ PM
IMAGE #				

SHOOTING MODE		METER MODE		
ISO		EV +/-		
WB		LENS		VR ○ ON ○ OFF
APERTURE		FOCAL LENGTH		
SHUTTER SPEED		FLASH	○ YES ○ NO	
TRIPOD	○ YES ○ NO	FLASH SETTINGS		

IN CAMERA SETTINGS	WEATHER

LIGHTING DESCRIPTION

SHOT NOTES

PHOTOGRAPHY LOGBOOK

DATE		TIME		○ AM ○ PM
IMAGE #				

SHOOTING MODE		METER MODE		
ISO		EV +/-		
WB		LENS		VR ○ ON ○ OFF
APERTURE		FOCAL LENGTH		
SHUTTER SPEED		FLASH	○ YES ○ NO	
TRIPOD	○ YES ○ NO	FLASH SETTINGS		

IN CAMERA SETTINGS	WEATHER

LIGHTING DESCRIPTION

SHOT NOTES

PHOTOGRAPHY LOGBOOK

DATE		TIME		○ AM ○ PM
IMAGE #				

SHOOTING MODE		METER MODE		
ISO		EV +/-		
WB		LENS		VR ○ ON ○ OFF
APERTURE		FOCAL LENGTH		
SHUTTER SPEED		FLASH	○ YES ○ NO	
TRIPOD	○ YES ○ NO	FLASH SETTINGS		

IN CAMERA SETTINGS	WEATHER

LIGHTING DESCRIPTION

SHOT NOTES

PHOTOGRAPHY LOGBOOK

DATE		TIME		○ AM ○ PM
IMAGE #				

SHOOTING MODE		METER MODE		
ISO		EV +/−		
WB		LENS		VR ○ ON ○ OFF
APERTURE		FOCAL LENGTH		
SHUTTER SPEED		FLASH	○ YES ○ NO	
TRIPOD	○ YES ○ NO	FLASH SETTINGS		

IN CAMERA SETTINGS	WEATHER

LIGHTING DESCRIPTION

SHOT NOTES

PHOTOGRAPHY LOGBOOK

DATE		TIME		○ AM ○ PM
IMAGE #				

SHOOTING MODE		METER MODE		
ISO		EV +/-		
WB		LENS	VR	○ ON ○ OFF
APERTURE		FOCAL LENGTH		
SHUTTER SPEED		FLASH	○ YES ○ NO	
TRIPOD	○ YES ○ NO	FLASH SETTINGS		

IN CAMERA SETTINGS	WEATHER

LIGHTING DESCRIPTION

SHOT NOTES

PHOTOGRAPHY LOGBOOK

DATE		TIME		○ AM ○ PM
IMAGE #				

SHOOTING MODE		METER MODE			
ISO		EV +/-			
WB		LENS		VR	○ ON ○ OFF
APERTURE		FOCAL LENGTH			
SHUTTER SPEED		FLASH	○ YES ○ NO		
TRIPOD	○ YES ○ NO	FLASH SETTINGS			

IN CAMERA SETTINGS	WEATHER

LIGHTING DESCRIPTION

SHOT NOTES

PHOTOGRAPHY LOGBOOK

DATE		TIME		○ AM ○ PM
IMAGE #				

SHOOTING MODE		METER MODE		
ISO		EV +/-		
WB		LENS		VR ○ ON ○ OFF
APERTURE		FOCAL LENGTH		
SHUTTER SPEED		FLASH	○ YES ○ NO	
TRIPOD	○ YES ○ NO	FLASH SETTINGS		

IN CAMERA SETTINGS	WEATHER

LIGHTING DESCRIPTION

SHOT NOTES

PHOTOGRAPHY LOGBOOK

DATE		TIME		○ AM ○ PM
IMAGE #				

SHOOTING MODE		METER MODE			
ISO		EV +/-			
WB		LENS		VR	○ ON ○ OFF
APERTURE		FOCAL LENGTH			
SHUTTER SPEED		FLASH	○ YES ○ NO		
TRIPOD	○ YES ○ NO	FLASH SETTINGS			

IN CAMERA SETTINGS	WEATHER

LIGHTING DESCRIPTION

SHOT NOTES

PHOTOGRAPHY LOGBOOK

DATE		TIME		○ AM ○ PM
IMAGE #				

SHOOTING MODE		METER MODE		
ISO		EV +/-		
WB		LENS	VR	○ ON ○ OFF
APERTURE		FOCAL LENGTH		
SHUTTER SPEED		FLASH	○ YES ○ NO	
TRIPOD	○ YES ○ NO	FLASH SETTINGS		

IN CAMERA SETTINGS	WEATHER

LIGHTING DESCRIPTION

SHOT NOTES

PHOTOGRAPHY LOGBOOK

DATE		TIME		○ AM ○ PM
IMAGE #				

SHOOTING MODE		METER MODE		
ISO		EV +/-		
WB		LENS	VR	○ ON ○ OFF
APERTURE		FOCAL LENGTH		
SHUTTER SPEED		FLASH	○ YES ○ NO	
TRIPOD	○ YES ○ NO	FLASH SETTINGS		

IN CAMERA SETTINGS	WEATHER

LIGHTING DESCRIPTION

SHOT NOTES

PHOTOGRAPHY LOGBOOK

DATE		TIME		○ AM ○ PM
IMAGE #				

SHOOTING MODE		METER MODE			
ISO		EV +/-			
WB		LENS		VR	○ ON ○ OFF
APERTURE		FOCAL LENGTH			
SHUTTER SPEED		FLASH	○ YES ○ NO		
TRIPOD	○ YES ○ NO	FLASH SETTINGS			

IN CAMERA SETTINGS	WEATHER

LIGHTING DESCRIPTION

SHOT NOTES

PHOTOGRAPHY LOGBOOK

DATE		TIME		○ AM ○ PM
IMAGE #				

SHOOTING MODE		METER MODE			
ISO		EV +/-			
WB		LENS		VR	○ ON ○ OFF
APERTURE		FOCAL LENGTH			
SHUTTER SPEED		FLASH	○ YES ○ NO		
TRIPOD	○ YES ○ NO	FLASH SETTINGS			

IN CAMERA SETTINGS	WEATHER

LIGHTING DESCRIPTION

SHOT NOTES

PHOTOGRAPHY LOGBOOK

DATE		TIME		○ AM ○ PM
IMAGE #				

SHOOTING MODE		METER MODE		
ISO		EV +/-		
WB		LENS		VR ○ ON ○ OFF
APERTURE		FOCAL LENGTH		
SHUTTER SPEED		FLASH	○ YES ○ NO	
TRIPOD	○ YES ○ NO	FLASH SETTINGS		

IN CAMERA SETTINGS	WEATHER

LIGHTING DESCRIPTION

SHOT NOTES

PHOTOGRAPHY LOGBOOK

DATE		TIME		○ AM ○ PM
IMAGE #				

SHOOTING MODE		METER MODE		
ISO		EV +/-		
WB		LENS		VR ○ ON ○ OFF
APERTURE		FOCAL LENGTH		
SHUTTER SPEED		FLASH	○ YES ○ NO	
TRIPOD	○ YES ○ NO	FLASH SETTINGS		

IN CAMERA SETTINGS

WEATHER

LIGHTING DESCRIPTION

SHOT NOTES

PHOTOGRAPHY LOGBOOK

DATE		TIME		○ AM ○ PM
IMAGE #				

SHOOTING MODE		METER MODE		
ISO		EV +/-		
WB		LENS		VR ○ ON ○ OFF
APERTURE		FOCAL LENGTH		
SHUTTER SPEED		FLASH	○ YES ○ NO	
TRIPOD	○ YES ○ NO	FLASH SETTINGS		

IN CAMERA SETTINGS	WEATHER

LIGHTING DESCRIPTION

SHOT NOTES

PHOTOGRAPHY LOGBOOK

DATE		TIME		○ AM ○ PM
IMAGE #				

SHOOTING MODE		METER MODE		
ISO		EV +/-		
WB		LENS	VR	○ ON ○ OFF
APERTURE		FOCAL LENGTH		
SHUTTER SPEED		FLASH	○ YES ○ NO	
TRIPOD	○ YES ○ NO	FLASH SETTINGS		

IN CAMERA SETTINGS	WEATHER

LIGHTING DESCRIPTION

SHOT NOTES

PHOTOGRAPHY LOGBOOK

DATE		TIME		○ AM ○ PM
IMAGE #				

SHOOTING MODE		METER MODE		
ISO		EV +/-		
WB		LENS		VR ○ ON ○ OFF
APERTURE		FOCAL LENGTH		
SHUTTER SPEED		FLASH	○ YES ○ NO	
TRIPOD	○ YES ○ NO	FLASH SETTINGS		

IN CAMERA SETTINGS	WEATHER

LIGHTING DESCRIPTION

SHOT NOTES

PHOTOGRAPHY LOGBOOK

DATE		TIME		○ AM ○ PM
IMAGE #				

SHOOTING MODE		METER MODE		
ISO		EV +/-		
WB		LENS		VR ○ ON ○ OFF
APERTURE		FOCAL LENGTH		
SHUTTER SPEED		FLASH	○ YES ○ NO	
TRIPOD	○ YES ○ NO	FLASH SETTINGS		

IN CAMERA SETTINGS	WEATHER

LIGHTING DESCRIPTION

SHOT NOTES

PHOTOGRAPHY LOGBOOK

DATE		TIME		○ AM ○ PM
IMAGE #				

SHOOTING MODE		METER MODE			
ISO		EV +/-			
WB		LENS		VR	○ ON ○ OFF
APERTURE		FOCAL LENGTH			
SHUTTER SPEED		FLASH	○ YES ○ NO		
TRIPOD	○ YES ○ NO	FLASH SETTINGS			

IN CAMERA SETTINGS	WEATHER

LIGHTING DESCRIPTION

SHOT NOTES

PHOTOGRAPHY LOGBOOK

DATE		TIME		○ AM ○ PM
IMAGE #				

SHOOTING MODE		METER MODE	
ISO		EV +/-	
WB		LENS	VR ○ ON ○ OFF
APERTURE		FOCAL LENGTH	
SHUTTER SPEED		FLASH	○ YES ○ NO
TRIPOD	○ YES ○ NO	FLASH SETTINGS	

IN CAMERA SETTINGS	WEATHER

LIGHTING DESCRIPTION

SHOT NOTES

PHOTOGRAPHY LOGBOOK

DATE		TIME		○ AM ○ PM
IMAGE #				

SHOOTING MODE		METER MODE		
ISO		EV +/-		
WB		LENS		VR ○ ON ○ OFF
APERTURE		FOCAL LENGTH		
SHUTTER SPEED		FLASH	○ YES ○ NO	
TRIPOD	○ YES ○ NO	FLASH SETTINGS		

IN CAMERA SETTINGS	WEATHER

LIGHTING DESCRIPTION

SHOT NOTES

PHOTOGRAPHY LOGBOOK

DATE		TIME		○ AM ○ PM
IMAGE #				

SHOOTING MODE		METER MODE	
ISO		EV +/−	
WB		LENS	VR ○ ON ○ OFF
APERTURE		FOCAL LENGTH	
SHUTTER SPEED		FLASH	○ YES ○ NO
TRIPOD	○ YES ○ NO	FLASH SETTINGS	

IN CAMERA SETTINGS	WEATHER

LIGHTING DESCRIPTION

SHOT NOTES

PHOTOGRAPHY LOGBOOK

DATE		TIME		○ AM ○ PM
IMAGE #				

SHOOTING MODE		METER MODE	
ISO		EV +/-	
WB		LENS	VR ○ ON ○ OFF
APERTURE		FOCAL LENGTH	
SHUTTER SPEED		FLASH	○ YES ○ NO
TRIPOD	○ YES ○ NO	FLASH SETTINGS	

IN CAMERA SETTINGS	WEATHER

LIGHTING DESCRIPTION

SHOT NOTES

PHOTOGRAPHY LOGBOOK

DATE		TIME		○ AM ○ PM
IMAGE #				

SHOOTING MODE		METER MODE		
ISO		EV +/-		
WB		LENS		VR ○ ON ○ OFF
APERTURE		FOCAL LENGTH		
SHUTTER SPEED		FLASH	○ YES ○ NO	
TRIPOD	○ YES ○ NO	FLASH SETTINGS		

IN CAMERA SETTINGS	WEATHER

LIGHTING DESCRIPTION

SHOT NOTES

PHOTOGRAPHY LOGBOOK

DATE		TIME		○ AM ○ PM
IMAGE #				

SHOOTING MODE		METER MODE		
ISO		EV +/-		
WB		LENS		VR ○ ON ○ OFF
APERTURE		FOCAL LENGTH		
SHUTTER SPEED		FLASH	○ YES ○ NO	
TRIPOD	○ YES ○ NO	FLASH SETTINGS		

IN CAMERA SETTINGS	WEATHER

LIGHTING DESCRIPTION

SHOT NOTES

PHOTOGRAPHY LOGBOOK

DATE		TIME		○ AM ○ PM
IMAGE #				

SHOOTING MODE		METER MODE			
ISO		EV +/-			
WB		LENS		VR	○ ON ○ OFF
APERTURE		FOCAL LENGTH			
SHUTTER SPEED		FLASH	○ YES ○ NO		
TRIPOD	○ YES ○ NO	FLASH SETTINGS			

IN CAMERA SETTINGS	WEATHER

LIGHTING DESCRIPTION

SHOT NOTES

PHOTOGRAPHY LOGBOOK

DATE		TIME		○ AM ○ PM
IMAGE #				

SHOOTING MODE		METER MODE		
ISO		EV +/-		
WB		LENS		VR ○ ON ○ OFF
APERTURE		FOCAL LENGTH		
SHUTTER SPEED		FLASH	○ YES ○ NO	
TRIPOD	○ YES ○ NO	FLASH SETTINGS		

IN CAMERA SETTINGS	WEATHER

LIGHTING DESCRIPTION

SHOT NOTES

PHOTOGRAPHY LOGBOOK

DATE		TIME		○ AM ○ PM
IMAGE #				

SHOOTING MODE		METER MODE		
ISO		EV +/-		
WB		LENS		VR ○ ON ○ OFF
APERTURE		FOCAL LENGTH		
SHUTTER SPEED		FLASH	○ YES ○ NO	
TRIPOD	○ YES ○ NO	FLASH SETTINGS		

IN CAMERA SETTINGS	WEATHER

LIGHTING DESCRIPTION

SHOT NOTES

PHOTOGRAPHY LOGBOOK

DATE		TIME	○ AM ○ PM
IMAGE #			

SHOOTING MODE		METER MODE			
ISO		EV +/-			
WB		LENS		VR	○ ON ○ OFF
APERTURE		FOCAL LENGTH			
SHUTTER SPEED		FLASH	○ YES ○ NO		
TRIPOD	○ YES ○ NO	FLASH SETTINGS			

IN CAMERA SETTINGS	WEATHER

LIGHTING DESCRIPTION

SHOT NOTES

PHOTOGRAPHY LOGBOOK

DATE		TIME		○ AM ○ PM
IMAGE #				

SHOOTING MODE		METER MODE			
ISO		EV +/-			
WB		LENS		VR	○ ON ○ OFF
APERTURE		FOCAL LENGTH			
SHUTTER SPEED		FLASH	○ YES ○ NO		
TRIPOD	○ YES ○ NO	FLASH SETTINGS			

IN CAMERA SETTINGS	WEATHER

LIGHTING DESCRIPTION

SHOT NOTES

PHOTOGRAPHY LOGBOOK

DATE		TIME		○ AM ○ PM
IMAGE #				

SHOOTING MODE		METER MODE		
ISO		EV +/-		
WB		LENS		VR ○ ON ○ OFF
APERTURE		FOCAL LENGTH		
SHUTTER SPEED		FLASH	○ YES ○ NO	
TRIPOD	○ YES ○ NO	FLASH SETTINGS		

IN CAMERA SETTINGS	WEATHER

LIGHTING DESCRIPTION

SHOT NOTES

PHOTOGRAPHY LOGBOOK

DATE		TIME		○ AM ○ PM
IMAGE #				

SHOOTING MODE		METER MODE		
ISO		EV +/-		
WB		LENS		VR ○ ON ○ OFF
APERTURE		FOCAL LENGTH		
SHUTTER SPEED		FLASH	○ YES ○ NO	
TRIPOD	○ YES ○ NO	FLASH SETTINGS		

IN CAMERA SETTINGS	WEATHER

LIGHTING DESCRIPTION

SHOT NOTES

PHOTOGRAPHY LOGBOOK

DATE		TIME		○ AM ○ PM
IMAGE #				

SHOOTING MODE		METER MODE		
ISO		EV +/-		
WB		LENS		VR ○ ON ○ OFF
APERTURE		FOCAL LENGTH		
SHUTTER SPEED		FLASH	○ YES ○ NO	
TRIPOD	○ YES ○ NO	FLASH SETTINGS		

IN CAMERA SETTINGS	WEATHER

LIGHTING DESCRIPTION

SHOT NOTES

PHOTOGRAPHY LOGBOOK

DATE		TIME		○ AM ○ PM
IMAGE #				

SHOOTING MODE		METER MODE		
ISO		EV +/-		
WB		LENS		VR ○ ON ○ OFF
APERTURE		FOCAL LENGTH		
SHUTTER SPEED		FLASH	○ YES ○ NO	
TRIPOD	○ YES ○ NO	FLASH SETTINGS		

IN CAMERA SETTINGS	WEATHER

LIGHTING DESCRIPTION

SHOT NOTES

PHOTOGRAPHY LOGBOOK

DATE		TIME		○ AM ○ PM
IMAGE #				

SHOOTING MODE		METER MODE	
ISO		EV +/-	
WB		LENS	VR ○ ON ○ OFF
APERTURE		FOCAL LENGTH	
SHUTTER SPEED		FLASH	○ YES ○ NO
TRIPOD	○ YES ○ NO	FLASH SETTINGS	

IN CAMERA SETTINGS	WEATHER

LIGHTING DESCRIPTION

SHOT NOTES

PHOTOGRAPHY LOGBOOK

DATE		TIME		○ AM ○ PM
IMAGE #				

SHOOTING MODE		METER MODE		
ISO		EV +/-		
WB		LENS		VR ○ ON ○ OFF
APERTURE		FOCAL LENGTH		
SHUTTER SPEED		FLASH	○ YES ○ NO	
TRIPOD	○ YES ○ NO	FLASH SETTINGS		

IN CAMERA SETTINGS	WEATHER

LIGHTING DESCRIPTION

SHOT NOTES

PHOTOGRAPHY LOGBOOK

DATE		TIME		○ AM ○ PM
IMAGE #				

SHOOTING MODE		METER MODE		
ISO		EV +/-		
WB		LENS	VR	○ ON ○ OFF
APERTURE		FOCAL LENGTH		
SHUTTER SPEED		FLASH	○ YES ○ NO	
TRIPOD	○ YES ○ NO	FLASH SETTINGS		

IN CAMERA SETTINGS	WEATHER

LIGHTING DESCRIPTION

SHOT NOTES

PHOTOGRAPHY LOGBOOK

DATE		TIME		○ AM ○ PM
IMAGE #				

SHOOTING MODE		METER MODE		
ISO		EV +/-		
WB		LENS		VR ○ ON ○ OFF
APERTURE		FOCAL LENGTH		
SHUTTER SPEED		FLASH	○ YES ○ NO	
TRIPOD	○ YES ○ NO	FLASH SETTINGS		

IN CAMERA SETTINGS	WEATHER

LIGHTING DESCRIPTION

SHOT NOTES

PHOTOGRAPHY LOGBOOK

DATE		TIME	○ AM ○ PM
IMAGE #			

SHOOTING MODE		METER MODE			
ISO		EV +/-			
WB		LENS		VR	○ ON ○ OFF
APERTURE		FOCAL LENGTH			
SHUTTER SPEED		FLASH	○ YES ○ NO		
TRIPOD	○ YES ○ NO	FLASH SETTINGS			

IN CAMERA SETTINGS	WEATHER

LIGHTING DESCRIPTION

SHOT NOTES

PHOTOGRAPHY LOGBOOK

DATE		TIME		○ AM ○ PM
IMAGE #				

SHOOTING MODE		METER MODE	
ISO		EV +/-	
WB		LENS	VR ○ ON ○ OFF
APERTURE		FOCAL LENGTH	
SHUTTER SPEED		FLASH	○ YES ○ NO
TRIPOD	○ YES ○ NO	FLASH SETTINGS	

IN CAMERA SETTINGS	WEATHER

LIGHTING DESCRIPTION

SHOT NOTES

PHOTOGRAPHY LOGBOOK

DATE		TIME		○ AM ○ PM
IMAGE #				

SHOOTING MODE		METER MODE	
ISO		EV +/-	
WB		LENS	VR ○ ON ○ OFF
APERTURE		FOCAL LENGTH	
SHUTTER SPEED		FLASH	○ YES ○ NO
TRIPOD	○ YES ○ NO	FLASH SETTINGS	

IN CAMERA SETTINGS	WEATHER

LIGHTING DESCRIPTION

SHOT NOTES

PHOTOGRAPHY LOGBOOK

DATE		TIME		○ AM ○ PM
IMAGE #				

SHOOTING MODE		METER MODE		
ISO		EV +/−		
WB		LENS	VR	○ ON ○ OFF
APERTURE		FOCAL LENGTH		
SHUTTER SPEED		FLASH	○ YES ○ NO	
TRIPOD	○ YES ○ NO	FLASH SETTINGS		

IN CAMERA SETTINGS	WEATHER

LIGHTING DESCRIPTION

SHOT NOTES

PHOTOGRAPHY LOGBOOK

DATE		TIME		○ AM ○ PM
IMAGE #				

SHOOTING MODE		METER MODE			
ISO		EV +/-			
WB		LENS		VR	○ ON ○ OFF
APERTURE		FOCAL LENGTH			
SHUTTER SPEED		FLASH	○ YES ○ NO		
TRIPOD	○ YES ○ NO	FLASH SETTINGS			

IN CAMERA SETTINGS	WEATHER

LIGHTING DESCRIPTION

SHOT NOTES

PHOTOGRAPHY LOGBOOK

DATE		TIME		○ AM ○ PM
IMAGE #				

SHOOTING MODE		METER MODE		
ISO		EV +/-		
WB		LENS		VR ○ ON ○ OFF
APERTURE		FOCAL LENGTH		
SHUTTER SPEED		FLASH	○ YES ○ NO	
TRIPOD	○ YES ○ NO	FLASH SETTINGS		

IN CAMERA SETTINGS	WEATHER

LIGHTING DESCRIPTION

SHOT NOTES

PHOTOGRAPHY LOGBOOK

DATE		TIME		○ AM ○ PM
IMAGE #				

SHOOTING MODE		METER MODE		
ISO		EV +/-		
WB		LENS		VR ○ ON ○ OFF
APERTURE		FOCAL LENGTH		
SHUTTER SPEED		FLASH	○ YES ○ NO	
TRIPOD	○ YES ○ NO	FLASH SETTINGS		

IN CAMERA SETTINGS	WEATHER

LIGHTING DESCRIPTION

SHOT NOTES

PHOTOGRAPHY LOGBOOK

DATE		TIME		○ AM ○ PM
IMAGE #				

SHOOTING MODE		METER MODE		
ISO		EV +/-		
WB		LENS		VR ○ ON ○ OFF
APERTURE		FOCAL LENGTH		
SHUTTER SPEED		FLASH	○ YES ○ NO	
TRIPOD	○ YES ○ NO	FLASH SETTINGS		

IN CAMERA SETTINGS	WEATHER

LIGHTING DESCRIPTION

SHOT NOTES

PHOTOGRAPHY LOGBOOK

DATE		TIME		○ AM ○ PM
IMAGE #				

SHOOTING MODE		METER MODE			
ISO		EV +/-			
WB		LENS		VR	○ ON ○ OFF
APERTURE		FOCAL LENGTH			
SHUTTER SPEED		FLASH	○ YES ○ NO		
TRIPOD	○ YES ○ NO	FLASH SETTINGS			

IN CAMERA SETTINGS	WEATHER

LIGHTING DESCRIPTION

SHOT NOTES

PHOTOGRAPHY LOGBOOK

DATE		TIME		○ AM ○ PM
IMAGE #				

SHOOTING MODE		METER MODE			
ISO		EV +/-			
WB		LENS		VR	○ ON ○ OFF
APERTURE		FOCAL LENGTH			
SHUTTER SPEED		FLASH	○ YES ○ NO		
TRIPOD	○ YES ○ NO	FLASH SETTINGS			

IN CAMERA SETTINGS	WEATHER

LIGHTING DESCRIPTION

SHOT NOTES

PHOTOGRAPHY LOGBOOK

DATE		TIME		○ AM ○ PM
IMAGE #				

SHOOTING MODE		METER MODE		
ISO		EV +/-		
WB		LENS	VR	○ ON ○ OFF
APERTURE		FOCAL LENGTH		
SHUTTER SPEED		FLASH	○ YES ○ NO	
TRIPOD	○ YES ○ NO	FLASH SETTINGS		

IN CAMERA SETTINGS	WEATHER

LIGHTING DESCRIPTION

SHOT NOTES

PHOTOGRAPHY LOGBOOK

DATE		TIME		○ AM ○ PM
IMAGE #				

SHOOTING MODE		METER MODE		
ISO		EV +/-		
WB		LENS		VR ○ ON ○ OFF
APERTURE		FOCAL LENGTH		
SHUTTER SPEED		FLASH	○ YES ○ NO	
TRIPOD	○ YES ○ NO	FLASH SETTINGS		

IN CAMERA SETTINGS	WEATHER

LIGHTING DESCRIPTION

SHOT NOTES

PHOTOGRAPHY LOGBOOK

DATE		TIME		○ AM ○ PM
IMAGE #				

SHOOTING MODE		METER MODE		
ISO		EV +/-		
WB		LENS		VR ○ ON ○ OFF
APERTURE		FOCAL LENGTH		
SHUTTER SPEED		FLASH	○ YES ○ NO	
TRIPOD	○ YES ○ NO	FLASH SETTINGS		

IN CAMERA SETTINGS	WEATHER

LIGHTING DESCRIPTION

SHOT NOTES

PHOTOGRAPHY LOGBOOK

DATE		TIME		○ AM ○ PM
IMAGE #				

SHOOTING MODE		METER MODE	
ISO		EV +/-	
WB		LENS	VR ○ ON ○ OFF
APERTURE		FOCAL LENGTH	
SHUTTER SPEED		FLASH	○ YES ○ NO
TRIPOD	○ YES ○ NO	FLASH SETTINGS	

IN CAMERA SETTINGS	WEATHER

LIGHTING DESCRIPTION

SHOT NOTES

PHOTOGRAPHY LOGBOOK

DATE		TIME		○ AM ○ PM
IMAGE #				

SHOOTING MODE		METER MODE		
ISO		EV +/-		
WB		LENS		VR ○ ON ○ OFF
APERTURE		FOCAL LENGTH		
SHUTTER SPEED		FLASH	○ YES ○ NO	
TRIPOD	○ YES ○ NO	FLASH SETTINGS		

IN CAMERA SETTINGS	WEATHER

LIGHTING DESCRIPTION

SHOT NOTES

PHOTOGRAPHY LOGBOOK

DATE		TIME		○ AM ○ PM
IMAGE #				

SHOOTING MODE		METER MODE	
ISO		EV +/-	
WB		LENS	VR ○ ON ○ OFF
APERTURE		FOCAL LENGTH	
SHUTTER SPEED		FLASH	○ YES ○ NO
TRIPOD	○ YES ○ NO	FLASH SETTINGS	

IN CAMERA SETTINGS	WEATHER

LIGHTING DESCRIPTION

SHOT NOTES

PHOTOGRAPHY LOGBOOK

DATE		TIME		○ AM ○ PM
IMAGE #				

SHOOTING MODE		METER MODE			
ISO		EV +/–			
WB		LENS		VR	○ ON ○ OFF
APERTURE		FOCAL LENGTH			
SHUTTER SPEED		FLASH	○ YES ○ NO		
TRIPOD	○ YES ○ NO	FLASH SETTINGS			

IN CAMERA SETTINGS	WEATHER

LIGHTING DESCRIPTION

SHOT NOTES

PHOTOGRAPHY LOGBOOK

DATE		TIME		○ AM ○ PM
IMAGE #				

SHOOTING MODE		METER MODE		
ISO		EV +/-		
WB		LENS		VR ○ ON ○ OFF
APERTURE		FOCAL LENGTH		
SHUTTER SPEED		FLASH	○ YES ○ NO	
TRIPOD	○ YES ○ NO	FLASH SETTINGS		

IN CAMERA SETTINGS	WEATHER

LIGHTING DESCRIPTION

SHOT NOTES

PHOTOGRAPHY LOGBOOK

DATE		TIME		○ AM ○ PM
IMAGE #				

SHOOTING MODE		METER MODE	
ISO		EV +/-	
WB		LENS	VR ○ ON ○ OFF
APERTURE		FOCAL LENGTH	
SHUTTER SPEED		FLASH	○ YES ○ NO
TRIPOD	○ YES ○ NO	FLASH SETTINGS	

IN CAMERA SETTINGS	WEATHER

LIGHTING DESCRIPTION

SHOT NOTES

PHOTOGRAPHY LOGBOOK

DATE		TIME		○ AM ○ PM
IMAGE #				

SHOOTING MODE		METER MODE		
ISO		EV +/-		
WB		LENS		VR ○ ON ○ OFF
APERTURE		FOCAL LENGTH		
SHUTTER SPEED		FLASH	○ YES ○ NO	
TRIPOD	○ YES ○ NO	FLASH SETTINGS		

IN CAMERA SETTINGS	WEATHER

LIGHTING DESCRIPTION

SHOT NOTES

PHOTOGRAPHY LOGBOOK

DATE		TIME		○ AM ○ PM
IMAGE #				

SHOOTING MODE		METER MODE	
ISO		EV +/-	
WB		LENS	VR ○ ON ○ OFF
APERTURE		FOCAL LENGTH	
SHUTTER SPEED		FLASH	○ YES ○ NO
TRIPOD	○ YES ○ NO	FLASH SETTINGS	

IN CAMERA SETTINGS	WEATHER

LIGHTING DESCRIPTION

SHOT NOTES

PHOTOGRAPHY LOGBOOK

DATE		TIME		○ AM ○ PM
IMAGE #				

SHOOTING MODE		METER MODE	
ISO		EV +/-	
WB		LENS	VR ○ ON ○ OFF
APERTURE		FOCAL LENGTH	
SHUTTER SPEED		FLASH	○ YES ○ NO
TRIPOD	○ YES ○ NO	FLASH SETTINGS	

IN CAMERA SETTINGS	WEATHER

LIGHTING DESCRIPTION

SHOT NOTES

PHOTOGRAPHY LOGBOOK

DATE		TIME		○ AM ○ PM
IMAGE #				

SHOOTING MODE		METER MODE		
ISO		EV +/-		
WB		LENS		VR ○ ON ○ OFF
APERTURE		FOCAL LENGTH		
SHUTTER SPEED		FLASH	○ YES ○ NO	
TRIPOD	○ YES ○ NO	FLASH SETTINGS		

IN CAMERA SETTINGS	WEATHER

LIGHTING DESCRIPTION

SHOT NOTES

PHOTOGRAPHY LOGBOOK

DATE		TIME		○ AM ○ PM
IMAGE #				

SHOOTING MODE		METER MODE		
ISO		EV +/−		
WB		LENS		VR ○ ON ○ OFF
APERTURE		FOCAL LENGTH		
SHUTTER SPEED		FLASH	○ YES ○ NO	
TRIPOD	○ YES ○ NO	FLASH SETTINGS		

IN CAMERA SETTINGS	WEATHER

LIGHTING DESCRIPTION

SHOT NOTES

PHOTOGRAPHY LOGBOOK

DATE		TIME		○ AM ○ PM
IMAGE #				

SHOOTING MODE		METER MODE		
ISO		EV +/-		
WB		LENS	VR	○ ON ○ OFF
APERTURE		FOCAL LENGTH		
SHUTTER SPEED		FLASH	○ YES ○ NO	
TRIPOD	○ YES ○ NO	FLASH SETTINGS		

IN CAMERA SETTINGS	WEATHER

LIGHTING DESCRIPTION

SHOT NOTES

PHOTOGRAPHY LOGBOOK

DATE		TIME		○ AM ○ PM
IMAGE #				

SHOOTING MODE		METER MODE	
ISO		EV +/-	
WB		LENS	VR ○ ON ○ OFF
APERTURE		FOCAL LENGTH	
SHUTTER SPEED		FLASH	○ YES ○ NO
TRIPOD	○ YES ○ NO	FLASH SETTINGS	

IN CAMERA SETTINGS	WEATHER

LIGHTING DESCRIPTION

SHOT NOTES

PHOTOGRAPHY LOGBOOK

DATE		TIME		○ AM ○ PM
IMAGE #				

SHOOTING MODE		METER MODE			
ISO		EV +/−			
WB		LENS		VR	○ ON ○ OFF
APERTURE		FOCAL LENGTH			
SHUTTER SPEED		FLASH	○ YES ○ NO		
TRIPOD	○ YES ○ NO	FLASH SETTINGS			

IN CAMERA SETTINGS	WEATHER

LIGHTING DESCRIPTION

SHOT NOTES

PHOTOGRAPHY LOGBOOK

DATE		TIME		○ AM ○ PM
IMAGE #				

SHOOTING MODE		METER MODE		
ISO		EV +/-		
WB		LENS		VR ○ ON ○ OFF
APERTURE		FOCAL LENGTH		
SHUTTER SPEED		FLASH	○ YES ○ NO	
TRIPOD	○ YES ○ NO	FLASH SETTINGS		

IN CAMERA SETTINGS	WEATHER

LIGHTING DESCRIPTION

SHOT NOTES

PHOTOGRAPHY LOGBOOK

DATE		TIME		○ AM ○ PM
IMAGE #				

SHOOTING MODE		METER MODE		
ISO		EV +/−		
WB		LENS		VR ○ ON ○ OFF
APERTURE		FOCAL LENGTH		
SHUTTER SPEED		FLASH	○ YES ○ NO	
TRIPOD	○ YES ○ NO	FLASH SETTINGS		

IN CAMERA SETTINGS	WEATHER

LIGHTING DESCRIPTION

SHOT NOTES